THE DOGS OF RON BURNS

A Tribute to the Dogs of 9/11

First Edition, 2014

Designed by Burns Studio Publishing, LLC
Photo documentation by Ira Schank and Cloudwatchers, LLC

ISBN 978-0-9725829-1-9

Published by Burns Studio Publishing, LLC
www.RonBurns.com

Printed and bound in the USA by O'Neil Printing, Phoenix, AZ

*Dedicated to all dogs that touch the hearts
and lives of people everyday.*

FOREWORD

I first saw Ron Burns' work when my brother, Brad, sent me the book, *The Dogs of Ron Burns*. In 2007, he was on a business trip in Scottsdale, Arizona and happened by a fine art gallery where some of Ron's pieces were on display. He was immediately drawn to Ron's work—the compelling subjects and the ordinary settings made extraordinary through color, composition and perspective. Brad felt a special connection to several of these dogs. It was there that he first saw "Sky," a black Labrador retriever with slightly crossed eyes and a joyous expression that shot straight to his heart. Chatting with the gallery owner, Brad was astounded to learn that Sky, whose full name is "Skyraider," was not only the portrait of a real dog, but one of the first canines to enter the Pentagon as part of a FEMA team from Maryland on September 11, 2001, while it was still burning and full of smoke. He called me that night to tell me about this amazing find. He couldn't wait for me to see Ron's work. "What are the odds?" he asked. I knew exactly what he meant: what were the chances that he would walk into a random art gallery so far from his home in Los Angeles and look into the soulful eyes of a hero dog who had responded to the Pentagon on our family's darkest day, six years earlier.

Knowing that our loved ones were lost somewhere in the chaos and being unable to help them or even get to them was one of the most agonizing aspects of 9/11 for the families of the victims. Years later, it is still comforting to see Sky and know that she had been there for our brother, Chic, when we could not be. As part of MD-Task Force 1, Sky worked tirelessly for three days of 12 hour shifts, wading through shoulder-deep water and dangerous material. She was a member of one of five Urban Search and Rescue teams deployed to the Pentagon. Twenty-one SAR teams responded to the World Trade Center. In all, some 250 to 300 K-9 teams worked the three attack sites, including the Staten Island sorting operation where cadaver dogs subsequently searched for human remains amid twisted steel and concrete. These are the unsung heroes who helped provide some closure for so many stunned and heartbroken families.

But search and rescue dogs weren't the only Best Friends we turned to on 9/11. I vividly remember the scene at the Family Assistance Center set up by the

"There is a special place in heaven for the dogs who perform the miracle of making a crying child smile."

Debra Burlingame

Department of Defense at the Sheraton Hotel across the street from the Pentagon. One at a time, families were ushered into a small conference room and given an excruciating briefing by military officers. They informed us of the conditions at the Pentagon and what we could expect regarding our loved ones' remains. Unbeknownst to us, waiting outside that room were volunteers with trained therapy dogs ready to go to work. There is a special place in heaven for the dogs who perform the miracle of making a crying child smile. I would never have believed the emotional comfort therapy dogs can provide under these dire circumstances had I not experienced it myself.

The fact that an artist as talented as Ron Burns has devoted his career to these special animals speaks to the kind of man he is and the passion that fuels his work. Ron's portraits capture the personalities of these dogs better than photographs. I have seen a photograph of Sirius, the NYPD Bomb Unit K-9 who was killed in the South Tower collapse. The photograph is a reminder of his dedication and fills me with gratitude, but Ron's portrait of Sirius, like Sky's, fills me with happiness. This is the essence of Ron's dogs; one looks at them and smiles. Three of Ron's 9/11 K-9 portraits are hung in my house and greet me every morning. How fitting that Sirius's portrait was selected to be a part of the historical exhibition in the National September 11 Memorial Museum at the World Trade Center.

I am deeply grateful to Ron for devoting a book to the dogs of 9/11. So much of our daily experience still returns us to the pain and anguish of that day, but Ron's work elicits memories of human decency, sacrifice and compassion triumphing over depravity. His paintings are a reminder of the great contribution to humankind made by the humblest of God's creatures. Ron's work is a celebration of life, goodness and abiding friendship.

Debra Burlingame
Sister of Capt. Charles F. "Chic" Burlingame, III
Pilot, American Airlines flight 77
Pentagon attack,
September 11, 2001
Hudson River Valley, NY
March 30, 2014

INTRODUCTION

The story of people and dogs is very old, going back tens of thousands of years. At some point their story became ours and ours became theirs. Children instinctively see dogs as friends and adults become children around them.

Dogs share in every part of our lives from birth to death.

This book brings together, through a collection of paintings, the story of what happens with people and dogs around times of crisis.

Here you'll see furry friends, such as explosive detection dogs, who work to keep us safe, canines who work to rescue us in times of greatest need, and of course those, such as therapy dogs, who work so lovingly to make us whole again.

The traits we like to think of as human ideals – patience, tenacity, unconditional love, hard work, kindness and heroism – are found consistently in dogs, perhaps more consistently than in people (I'm biased).

And it's my hope that by seeing these gorgeous creatures through the lens of art, that we can all appreciate them and celebrate them in a new and profound way.

ACKNOWLEDGEMENTS

My sincerest thanks goes to everyone whose contributions made my paintings come to life.
I am grateful for the opportunity to share your stories.

Ron Burns

SIRIUS

Explosive Detection - Port Authority Police Department K9

On September 11th 2001, Sirius, an explosive detection dog working in Tower II of the World Trade Center, gave his life for his country. His responsibilities, along with his handler David Lim, included inspecting vehicles for explosives that entered the WTC. On September 11, 2001, Sirius and David were in their office in Tower II when they felt the first plane slam into Tower I. Lim left Sirius in the office promising to return. But while assisting in rescue operations Lim became trapped in a stairwell, along with a grandmother and firefighters from Ladder Company 6, for several hours when Tower I collapsed. Once freed he attempted to return to Tower II which was now rubble and inaccessible.

When Sirius' remains were removed from the World Trade Center wreckage, they were given the same honors accorded firefighters and other rescuers, who lost their lives there too.

SKY

Search and Rescue - FEMA

Sky, whose real name was Skyraider, was on the first reconnaissance team to enter the Pentagon on 9/11/01. There was still heavy fire and intense heat, but she went in focused on doing her job. She would search without me having to say a word. She is a small dog, but she has a big heart.

Bob Sessions

(Following page)

GUINNESS

Search and Rescue - Mountain View Dog Training

Guinness was my search partner for many years. He and I deployed to the WTC on 9/11, Hurricanes Katrina and Rita, La Conchita mudslide, Waterman Canyon mudslide and many wilderness searches for the San Bernardino Sheriff's Department.

He came from another service dog organization and was given to me when the trainer working with him saw that he had tremendous drive and focus for a toy. He would do anything for a chance to retrieve or tug with any toy! So he became a "career change" dog and absolutely excelled in search work.

He gave his all in everything I asked him to do, every time.

He was very devoted to me and watched my every move constantly. He was thrilled to get any opportunity to work!

He retired from search work when he was 10 but was still always willing to work. He patiently worked with new search dog handlers I trained and he enjoyed his retirement showing them how to handle a search dog!

We go on an annual family vacation to Shaver Lake and Guinness enjoyed that immensely. He loved to swim, boat and retrieve and went with us on that trip until he was 14 years old.

Sheila McKee

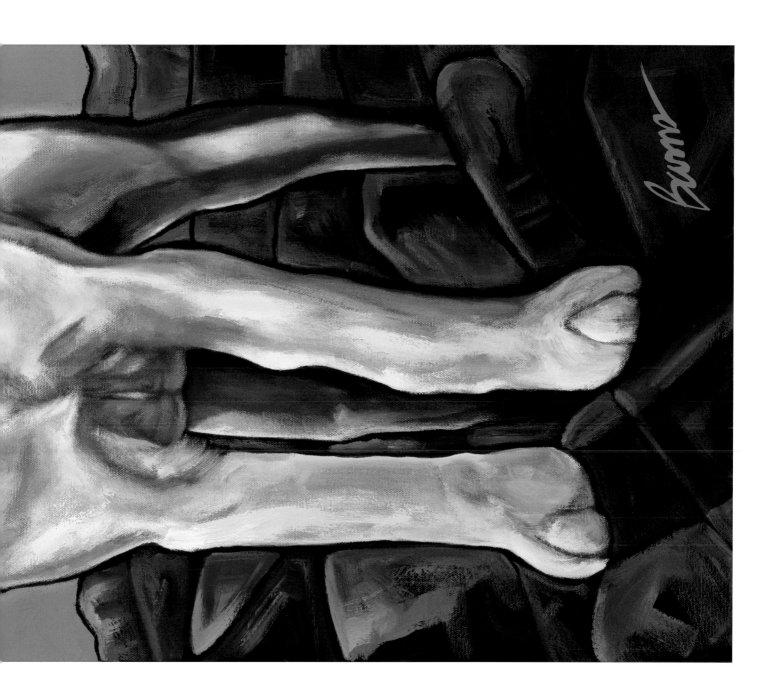

GERIN

Pet Therapy - Therapet

"I'd like to take him home. And the first thing I'd do is buy him a Harley vest." That would have been a sight I'd never imagined. But, looking at how Gerin was standing, projecting strength and steadiness, with his head in a rescuers lap, I could see it. We moved on, and he became both a playful puppy and "a dog that would protect my little sister" in the children's area. Gerin was there, calm and even, seeming to draw anxiety from the hands touching his fur into himself, providing enough calmness that questions could be answered, forms filled out. How he knew what each person needed was unknown, but he did, and never put a paw down wrong.

That was Gerin. A marvelous working dog who could summon whatever part of his personality was needed. He could go from playing Chewbacca at a Halloween party at a nursing home, to herding sheep, to an agility trial, to just talking to me without turning a hair – and he had many hairs that could be turned.

Gerin has passed on now. He was a very special dog who had a great instinct for the best response to each person he interacted with. He seemed to read that immediately. He could always make you feel that a new day was coming, and that no matter what sorrow or joys it carried, you'd manage just fine.

Marita Spooner

NERO

Search and Rescue - Fairfax Search Dogs

He was matted and skinny; he was also bold and confident, hitting 3 rungs as he bounded up a ladder to a shed roof and jumping down to the ground. He was happy to do anything for a toy, dunking his head in a bin of water to retrieve the ball, holding onto the ball on a string as the man lifted him off the ground and swung him around his shoulders. He was to be my new partner.

He looked at me and decided a home, after 17 months as a kennel dog in Slovakia, Germany, and rural NY State, might not be such a bad thing. While unloading my truck in 90 degree heat, unbeknownst to me, he jumped the fence and climbed back into the crate.

He learned household manners in a flash. I doubt he'd ever had toys and thus was never found without one – preferably two, so you always knew where he'd been.

He quickly learned his nose was the key to his payment whether it was on the rubble, in the woods, or on a search boat. In fact, in beginning Schutzhund he saw no reason to go around the blind as he was supposed to – he had gone up and sniffed and knew no one was there. He was intense in his work in a quiet, purposeful, clear-headed way, teaching himself to seek the high point on the rubble to better work the scent.

All he ever asked was to "work" and to be with us – kind of a lopsided bargain, it seems to me, but one for which I'm forever grateful.

December 25, 1997 – September 27, 2007

Elizabeth Kreitler

HAGRID

Autism Service Dog - Guiding Eyes for the Blind/Heeling Autism

Heeling Autism service dog Hagrid joined the Mandell family in April 2012. While his main role is to provide safety and companionship for the Mandells' youngest son, Sam, Hagrids' presence has benefited the entire family – mom and dad and their five boys. Once trapped in their home for fear of Sam getting hurt or lost, the family is now regularly out and about – traveling to malls and sporting events and taking family vacations. They've even been to Disney World three times since Hagrid's arrival! Perhaps Sam's brother put it best when he remarked on how wonderful it is for "one life to change seven."

Michelle Brier

TARA

Search and Rescue - MATF-1 USAR Team

Tara was a little black lab that came from Florida. I got Tara at the age of nine months. We joined the FEMA Urban Search and Rescue Team, Massachusetts Task Force 1 in the spring of 1996. Tara was trained to locate live survivors in wilderness search and in building collapses. She was first certified to the FEMA basic level in the spring of 1998. Tara received her FEMA advanced certification in the fall of 1998. Tara was an energetic partner that had a powerful play drive. She loved the game of search and rescue and she was always eager to please. Tara went on numerous wilderness searches and several building collapses. Tara's biggest mission was the attack on the World Trade Center.

Tara searched the World Trade Center rubble for eight days after the attacks. Through it all she stayed focused and alert and was always willing to search. Even though Tara did not find anyone during her eight days there, she brought comfort to all around her. Tara was a wonderful partner and fulfilled our lives with love till the day she passed away.

May you rest in peace my partner.
April 15, 1995 – March 25, 2011

Lee Prentiss

TIKVA

Pet Therapy - Hope Animal-Assisted Crisis Response

Some men are sitting in chairs, others on 5 gallon buckets staring as their comrades sift carefully through debris, hoping for any sign of life. No one is talking. A multitude of expressions sweep over their dirt stained faces as we approach one of the many stations around the "pile". When they find out that the dogs are brought in to see them, some joke, others ask what it is that the dogs do. I make my way towards them and ask Tikva to go say "hi." Her enthusiasm changes to calm. She becomes keen on making her way towards a man sitting and staring at the pile. She touches her nose to his knee, as he reaches out to pat her, she lifts her paws up towards his lap as if she too is reaching. He carefully lifts her into his lap and is surprised to feel the softness of her fur. She tucks her face into the crook of his arm and waits for his fingers to massage her. Perhaps she too is seeking comfort. We remain at this site for about 2 hours. Conversation is lighthearted with one while another strokes Tikva's fur, sharing about his experience of the last 12 days.

WTC site Sept 23, 2001- Journal account of Animal
Assisted Crisis Response 2001

The mayor's office asked us to accompany families on the Ferry Boats. We would go to the site for part of the day, then to VMAT for decontamination and then make our way to the Family Assistance Center to accompany a family. A woman waiting to board the ferry boat reaches towards Tikva. "I can't believe you are here," she whispers. As Tikva draws closer, the woman leans over, reaches toward her and begins to hug her, burying her face deeper into the fur on her neck and begins to cry. She looked at her badge and said, "her name is Tikva, that means Hope in Hebrew and I am Jewish". She makes the comment that her husband loved dogs more than anything except her and that he had a merle blue collie. She thinks Tikva looks like his dog before they got together. She remarks that this thing that just happened is a gift to her husband and a sign to give her hope and strength.

Family Assistance Center Pier 94 Sept. 2001

Cindy Ehlers
Founder - Hope Animal-Assisted Crisis Response

OTTO

Search and Rescue - Virginia Task Force 1

Otto was a dog that captured your heart, whether you're a rescue worker, a family member or a handler — you remembered him. Otto was "honorable", athletic and driven. As you watched him search, you knew he "had to know the answer" as much as anyone. Otto set the bar for me. When we finished a search, no matter what the scenario, we knew that no one was left behind. I was the luckiest handler in the world. My first dog turned out to be a superstar. That is rare.

As the lead canine trainer of the National Disaster Search Dog Foundation, all of our dogs must be superstars. Nothing else is acceptable. The victims and families deserve it. This is not a sport, it's life or death. Long live Otto. My boy. Peace.

Sonja Heritage
Lead Canine Trainer
National Disaster Search Dog Foundation

ANNIE

Pet Therapy - Delta Society

Some dogs retrieve tennis balls, Annie retrieves trust; some dogs herd sheep, Annie herds hope. Annie made over 20 visits to Ground Zero.

Liz Teal
Founder - Giving Paws

(Following page)

ROSELLE

Guide Dog - Guide Dogs for the Blind

On September 11, 2001 Roselle and I were in our office on the 78th floor of Tower One of the World Trade Center when the tower was struck by American Airlines flight 11 which had been hijacked and was being controlled by terrorists. Working as a team, Roselle led myself along with the others on our floor, down the darkened stairwell (that consisted of 1,463 steps) to safety moments before the building collapsed. She remained poised and calm through the entire day. She gave kisses and love wherever she could and she worked when she needed to do so. I would not be alive today if it weren't for Roselle. I cannot say enough about the incredible job she did. What Roselle did on 9/11 is a testimony not only to the Stern's and the others who raised her, but also to her trainer, Todd Jurek, the entire GDB training staff, and all the people who make up the wonderful organization of Guide Dogs for the Blind. Most of all, what Roselle did that day and in fact every day she and I were together is nothing less than the strongest possible evidence I can provide of the value of teamwork and trust.

Roselle was unique without a doubt. She worked through the most trying time in our nation's history, and she was right there unflinching for all of it. Her spirit never diminished and, in fact, grew stronger through the years after 9/11 which helps me be a better person today. I thank God for the time Karen and I were allowed to have the wonderful creature which was Roselle with us. She touched everyone whom she met and I'm sure everyone's path she crossed is better for knowing her. She kissed firefighters in the World Trade Center as we descended the stairs. She gave unconditional love to so many people wherever she went. She inspired us all and will continue to do so.

Michael Hingson
Roselle's Dream Foundation

WUSEL

Pet Therapy - Therapy Dogs International

Wusel was a rescue from a municipal shelter. We had finally decided to have another dog after we had lost our last GSD. As we walked by all those cages it was not easy to select one dog. I will never forget, all those poor dogs in the need of a loving home. Wusel was sitting there in his cage and I realized that he was still a puppy. We took him out for a walk and we saw that he was a very sweet people-oriented dog and had the kind of temperament needed to be a therapy dog. His estimated age was six months. He went through the therapy dog test when he was just about a year old. At the time of 9/11 he was 1 1/2 years old. He did absolutely fabulous work, especially with the children. Since I am in charge of Therapy Dogs International I visited almost every second day for the times our dogs were scheduled. This was extremely hard and tiring for Wusel, yet he gave his all. So many people wanted to see him. He did make such a difference. So much so that one of the young America Corps workers wrote a poem about the therapy dogs but dedicated it to her special friend Wusel and the other therapy dogs. I can honestly say that he helped innumerable people and made them feel better for at least a little while. He had the ability to make people laugh and subsequently they could cry. He was the kind of dog who interacted by sitting in front and totally concentrated on the person he was visiting with. This is something one cannot teach a dog this is the behavior of a therapy dog born, not made.

We were privileged to have had him in our lives even if it was for an all too short time. He will be missed forever.

Ursula Kempe
President - Therapy Dogs International

EVEREST

Search and Rescue - FEMA

Reeny and Everest had just finished their night shift on the pile in NYC when, as they were stepping out of the rubble field, Everest stopped short and seemed to be sniffing and focused very heavily on a piece of paper on the ground. Reeny went over and picked it up and it was a business card. Everest seemed very intent on smelling the card. Reeny didn't think anything of it but had it in her pocket when she came home to Arizona from the deployment. We got to talking about that event as kind of a debrief to the whole deployment and we decided to look up the name on the card and found that his memorial was planned and there was an address for his wife. Reeny wrote a letter to her stating that Everest had focused on this card and that Reeny felt it was important for her to know that while she and Everest were not able to find anyone alive that finding this card brought home why she went which was to find a remembrance at least of her husband. His wife wrote back thanking her and said that this was really the only thing tangible from the site (at that time) that she had that represented her loved one. So in the end, Reeny and Everest's mission was to find the card and get it back to his wife to help her heal.

Everest was a most special dog, Reeny loved her like her child. They were a special team.

Tom and Reeny Shannon

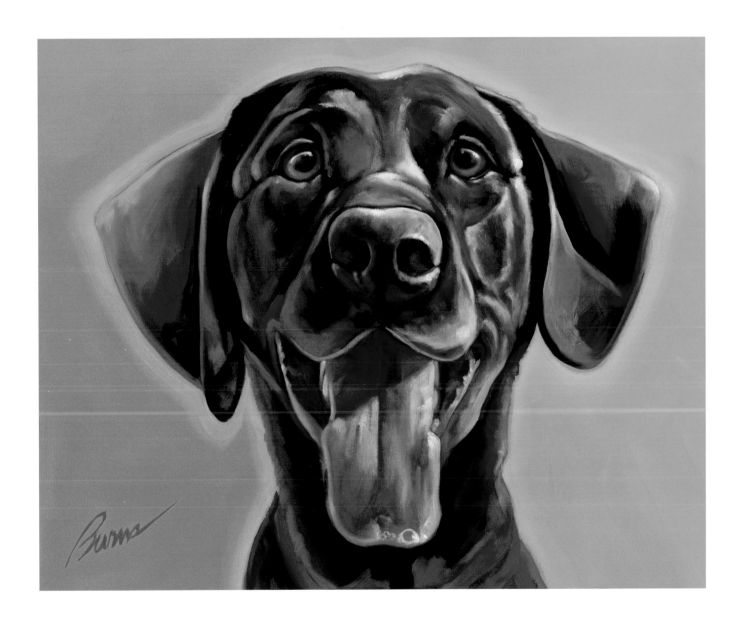

SHERIDAN

Search and Rescue - VA-TF1

As a member of VA-TF1, Sheridan and I were dispatched to the Pentagon on 9/11. We entered the building shortly after arriving and began searching for possible survivors who hadn't been pulled out by the initial response efforts. These beginning forays were somewhat limited due to a number of safety factors that put us at risk. For Sheridan, the risks included smoke inhalation (there was still a fair amount of smoke from the ongoing fire) and floors that were extremely hot in some areas and which were difficult to recognize since we were wearing large insulated boots. Large parts of the building were still collapsing and very unstable, so we couldn't penetrate those areas until they had been shored up. Toward the end of our week-long mission, it became apparent that the chance of finding any survivors was extremely unlikely, and some of the dogs started to be used to find the deceased. Sheridan participated in those efforts and did locate one deceased person. Although the Pentagon was his only FEMA deployment, Sheridan went on over 100 search missions through my local wilderness group. He had several finds during his career, the most notable being an arm bone that had a bullet hole in it; this prompted a lengthy homicide investigation that was eventually documented and aired in an episode on The Real NCIS, a Discovery Communications program.

Chris Holleyman

SARIAH, ZLATA AND RIVER

Search and Rescue - FEMA

After deciding to get a disaster dog I started looking in a multitude of places, including local shelters. I would go every 3 days and "test" any of the dogs that came in. After about 4 months and testing 50 dogs I was becoming discouraged. My wife was talking to a friend that had several dogs and she said she had a black lab that she wanted to give to a good home. The only thing was Sariah was very busy and needed to work or do something (PERFECT for ME). I "tested" Sariah several times and she passed with flying colors!

We are members of Arizona Task Force 1 which is part of the Urban Search & Rescue Team for the Federal Emergency Management Agency (FEMA). Sariah loved to retrieve anything, anywhere, anytime! She usually carried my shoes and duty boots around the house just to let me know she was ready to go to the Fire Department or rubble pile to work.

Scott Krushak

A local breeder who gifted a pup from each litter to rescue groups donated Zlata to the group and me as the handler. She was deployed to the Salt Lake Olympics in 2002. She was a "tom boy" but very efficient in her energy use. She would watch the others chase toys and wait for them to return before taking it from them.

River was donated to our search group by a fellow firefighter who breeds yellow labs. River was in a kennel for 5 months when her incredible "play drive" was noticed. River was very sweet, she loved to lie on top of us and be petted. River flew to Seattle with us on her first commercial flight in the cabin that is required for FEMA dogs. She was very popular and well behaved. If she had not been used as a working dog, she would have been left in a kennel, breeding her entire life. We loved her deeply.

Tom and Reeny Shannon

HANSEN

Search and Rescue - NYPD

It was 6 months after the attacks that K9 Hansen and I reported to Ground Zero for a 6 am to 6 pm tour. We were requested to respond for a search. So after driving the gator, with Hansen, to the search area, we climbed down 100 feet into a hole where Hansen located several victim remains. I rewarded him with "good boy, good job", letting him know he had done his job and we were done. Hansen ran up the hill ahead of me to get back into the gator.

I noticed him jump out and start to dig on the side of the road. By the time I got to him he had already dug a hole almost 1 foot down. Never in the six months there had I seen him act this way. Another emergency service officer came to see what we were doing. I said Hansen is going crazy so we all started digging. We went about 2 feet down and I was ready to call it off when we uncovered a G shock watch. The next shovel uncovered the arm that it was on. Any body part this big was very rare so we called for more officers to help. After a slow hand dig we realized it was a complete body. Then one of the officers found a gun. We reported the gun and they said we had recovered Officer Perry. Officer Perry was retiring on Sept. 11 and was at headquarters. He ran to the Trade Center after the first plane hit. This was a great recovery for the police department. Everyone talked about how Hansen had found Officer Perry. Then the Chief said they had good info that Sgt. Curtin was with Officer Perry. Hansen and I had worked many jobs with Sgt. Curtin. So once again I sent Hansen out and in about 2 minutes and about 3 feet away he started digging like crazy. We all looked at each other and said "no way". In a few hours we found a machine gun which was Sgt. Curtin's. His complete body was recovered. Even being able to read his name on his uniform. Sgt. Curtin had been a marine before becoming a police officer. He had helped dig out a marine that was killed in the Oklahoma City bombing. This was a proud day for me and Hansen to bring home 2 of our own.

Hansen, a Belgian Shepherd Dog, worked on site for approximately 150 days. He was honored with numerous awards for his service including a memorial statue at a local park in Lindenhurst, New York.

Steve Smaldon
NYPD

PATRICK

Pet Therapy - Therapet

On the first day of the Presentation of Flags and Urns, when families were presented with their loved ones ashes from Ground Zero, Patrick and I stood just outside the building's entrance working with the families who were waiting in line to enter. One woman in line reached for Patrick, then dropped to her knees and collapsed emotionally into him. While she was crying out her grief to him she would stop every so often and ask me for his name, then his age, make a comment or laugh at herself, then begin crying again. This continued for five or ten minutes. The harder she cried, the closer Patrick placed himself to her. A member of her family came back outside to find her. With a deep sigh she calmed herself and gave Patrick and me big hugs. She thanked us and told us that now she would be able to handle what she needed to do.

Elaine Shoe-Ezell

FIDEL

Pet Therapy - The Good Dog Foundation

Fidel, a Good Dog Foundation therapy dog, won honorable mention in the American Kennel Club's Awards for Canine Excellence in 2002, the ASPCA "Trooper" award and was one of three honored by the American Red Cross for outstanding service as a therapy dog in serving those affected by the 9/11 World Trade Center Tragedy - making over 9 visits to Ground Zero.

"Fidel's pitter patter on your leg opens your heart to receive his constant love."

Rachel McPherson
Founder - The Good Dog Foundation

MADISON

Search and Rescue - FEMA
(Following page)

Madi came to me on the 12th of December of 1998. By a chance encounter at a general obedience class we met a local Search Dog Team member who planted a seed. That, with a lot of perseverance, paid off in our certification as a FEMA Type 1 Advanced Disaster Search Team in February of 2002. We were Type 2 Basic for the 9/11 attacks, but we were not called up. Madi also trained for her Wilderness Certification.

Madi was a real sweetheart that went 200mph all the time. There was no medium or slow, only real fast. A daily swim kept her in top shape. She trained on average 35-40 hours a month. Madison was a wonderful dog who opened up a whole new world to me in Search and Rescue. Because of her I have found a special way to give back to my fellow man.

Peter Sellas

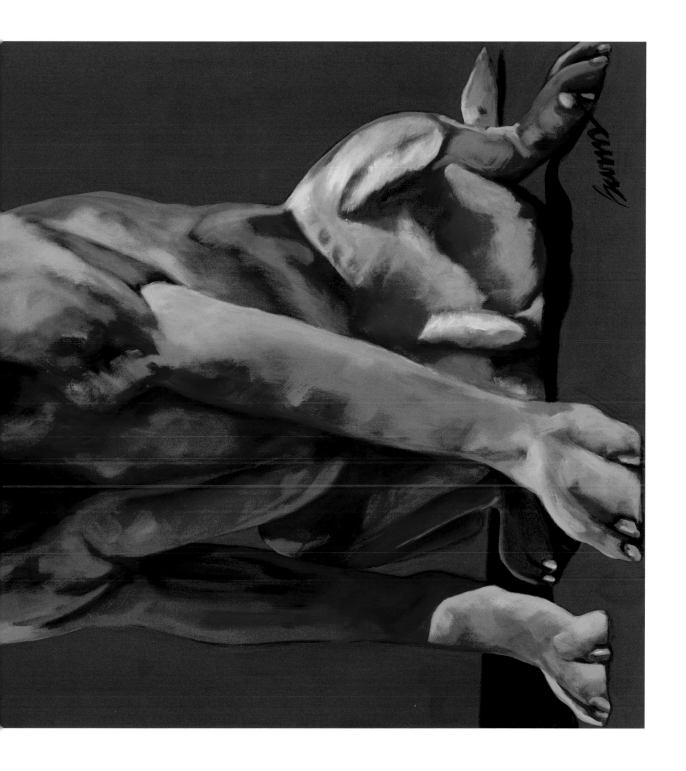

RED

Search and Rescue - FEMA

Red was a cross trained dog and very reliable in each using different commands. She searched for lost live people in the woods or under rubble and also specialized in cadaver detection. She had many finds over the years which included her work with archeologists with her finding a child's remains that were approximately 1,000 years old. She was a certified FEMA disaster dog, as well as certified by several different law enforcement agencies in cadaver work.

She was a mostly stoic faced dog. I called it her poker face, but when I asked her to search she came to life smiling & animated as she worked. She was a quirky dog but turned out to be super reliable in any situation. In all the years despite numerous disasters from 9/11 to Katrina to multistory fire scenes, she only got hurt once on a real mission. When she was 10 years old she was trying to get to a fire victim after his 3 story house was mostly gone and he was hidden under debris hanging precariously a story up over a smoldering pile below when the debris had a secondary collapse. She ended up hanging by her armpits on a deck beam and had to pull herself up and get to safety. A nail or other sharp object cut her leg to the bone and through a vein. Luckily she recovered fully from that incident and went on to work two more years.

She was usually a quiet passive dog, but when she was barking to indicate she found a live person she had the deepest, loudest strong bark. It didn't seem to match her small body. She would do anything I ever asked of her and was a pleasure to live and work with. I definitely miss her! Red passed away in April 2012 at the age of 13 and was cremated with her favorite toy duck.

Heather Roche

VALIK

Assistance Dog - Canine Companions for Independence

Brendan was born with severe cerebral palsy and has undergone eight major orthopedic surgeries. He requires an attendant and a wheelchair. Prior to Valik joining the family, Brendan was tactilely defensive (didn't like to be touched) but Valik has lovingly desensitized him by lying across his lap, kissing him and providing unconditional love and patience to "his person." Brendan's mom, Martie, tributes Valik in providing an emotional connection that supports the whole family. "Valik is Brendan's bridge into the community."

Martie Koskoff

DRAKO

Search and Rescue - Virginia Task Force 1

Drako was my teacher and "a teacher". He taught the value of disaster search dogs to first responders throughout the UK and strengthened their K9 program. He started the DCFD US&R K9 program and responded to all calls as the only FEMA certified Disaster K9 in the district for several years. He certified with several new handlers, teaching them what a FEMA dog should be. He was a technician. Drako raised my bar to another level. Precise and correct. Fast. Fun. Agile. Sharp. Enthusiastic. 100 mph. I knew, pulling up to any scene — that if someone was in there, Drako would find them and fast. Period.

What more can a handler say as a testament to their partner? Although he has passed on, I think about him often and get a big smile.

Sonja Heritage
Lead Canine Trainer
National Disaster Search Dog Foundation

MOLLY

Pet Therapy - Delta Society

We went to Ground Zero and the Piers three days a week for the entire time the Piers were open and a few extra days for special days and events. From the end of September until either April or May the following year we were there around 100 times. After that, she and I ended up doing several speeches for different events and Molly was honored in Washington DC for her service after the tragedy. Quite an event. Ali McGraw was the host and Molly gave her the biggest kiss ever. I think they became friends for life!

Molly continued to work at United Cerebral Palsy Center and later at St. Luke Hospital. She was also a model and appeared in several print ads for Hush Puppies, as well as Lenox China, Booda Velvets and a few others. She even did a Bounty TV commercial out at Silvercup Studios where she ended up running into James Gandolfini and charming HIM onto all fours....where he proceeded to play with her until his car arrived!

When my Mother become seriously ill in Ohio, I was fortunate to be able to arrange for Molly to accompany me to her hospital bed in Ohio - where Molly laid on her bed for hours and hours and brought endless joy to my Mom. To say she was a blessing is a HUGE understatement.

Sadly, Molly is no longer with us. I still cry when I think about her and how much I miss her.

Cate Pontoni

COBY

Search and Rescue - FEMA

Coby was adopted from the Redlands Humane Society in May of 1996, when he was about 14 months old. Sheila, who was training her Rottweiler Osa for Search and Rescue, saw some potential in Coby for a career in Search and Rescue. He became certified as a FEMA Type II Urban Search and Rescue Dog in November of 1997 and FEMA Type I Urban Search and Rescue Dog in November of 1998.

Coby's major deployment was to the World Trade Center on September 11, 2001. He worked for 10 nights on the pile and located approximately 20 human remains. Coby was not trained in Human Remains Detection, but his interest in the remains assisted in providing some closure for many families.

After returning from 9/11 Coby became certified in Human Remains Detection and responded to natural disasters and crime scenes to locate the remains of victims.

After his retirement from Search and Rescue he continued to enjoy swimming any chance he could get and his annual trip to Shaver Lake. He was always happiest along the shore of the lake retrieving rocks from under the water and stacking them up on shore.

Coby died suddenly from cardiovascular collapse on March 14, 2011 with Dave and Sheila by his side, he was 16 years old.

David Graves and Sheila McKee

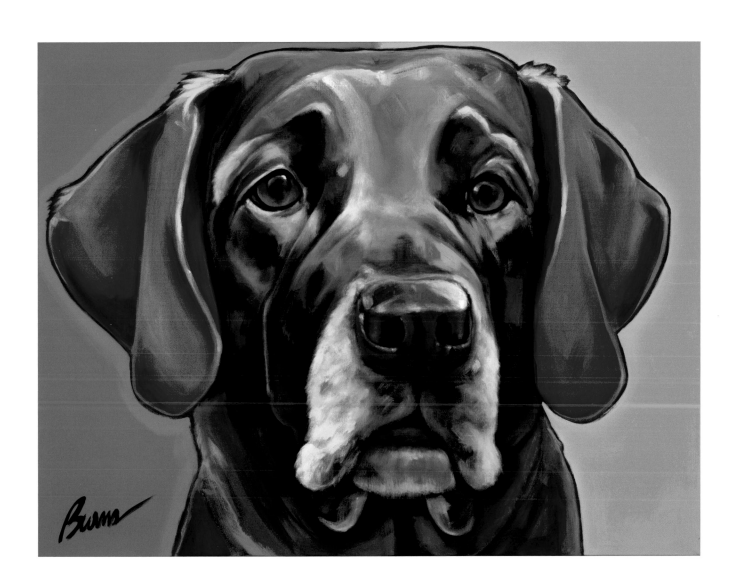

WOODY

Pet Therapy - Delta Society

Woody was a little street dog picked up off the streets somewhere outside of Newark, New Jersey. The shelter named him Woodrow - Woody for short. By fate, Woody and I came together. Woody was very special. He had a sense of humor and was fun to be with.

There was a police boat that left from the pier where the Family Assistance Center was and it took the victim's families down to Ground Zero. Woody went on that boat. I will never forget going. The silence was chilling. Families petted him with nervous anxiety as we sailed down to the site. People clung to Woody as we neared the dock. The site was eerie and felt holy at the same time. Woody led the people to the platform that overlooked the devastation past the military and police men and women standing like statues in tribute. The family members had their private time on the viewing platform and returned — some rushing to hug Woody as they headed back to the boat. Woody knew that his job was to be brave and to be strong for these grieving families and he was, and he did. He was probably hugged a little too tightly and grabbed at with too much vigor, but he welcomed the hugs and outreached arms and he responded to the need to be comforted. It was natural for him. He knew they needed him and he gave them the love and warmth they craved. He was proud and I could see it in his eyes as he looked back at me.

Woody went there twice a week for many months. He visited with old and young alike. The people would rush up to him and hug him and hold him. Some family members told Woody about their loved one. Some held him and wept. Others stroked him and wept in silence and others embraced him without saying a word and he knew what to do. I was so proud of this little guy from the street. I will never forget.

Woody, a stray dog who made a big difference in a lot of lives.

Lynne Lerner

SOPHIE

Pet Therapy - The Good Dog Foundation

Sophie was a six week old puppy when she was found by a NYC animal control officer. She was all alone in a drainage culvert in the Bronx, NY. She had an obsession with drainage pipes. I wonder if she was looking for her mother.

She failed her first temperament evaluation at the ASPCA and appeared on Good Morning America as an example of a puppy you should not adopt. But my granddaughter Lucy persuaded me to adopt her. She had confidence in Sophie and she was right. Slowly, her behavior improved as a result of being socialized by many loving and patient people at the ASPCA.

She was certified as a therapy dog by The Good Dog Foundation. She worked for years with a special group of people who had been convicted of animal cruelty. Some of these people had killed their own dog and it is very important that these people have a dog they can apologize to... a stand in for their animal victim.

Sophie made numerous visits to Ground Zero.

Stephanie Lafarge, Ph.D.

LEE

Service Dog - Canine Companions for Independence

I refer to Lee as Lee-Lee. I can tell you Lee is a true Diva. When she was actively working as my service dog, I referred to her as the mighty pulling machine. Some of my favorite memories are having Lee pull me through the streets of New York, specifically Chelsea Piers going lightning speed and her relentless obsession with picking up anything and everything that has been on the floor. She loves to greet people by carrying objects in her mouth. Needless to say, if I did not put my shoes away in the closet, I was guaranteed that one shoe would be at a different location, typically greeting a guest at my front door.

Lee retired as my service dog and is now continuing to work as a social companion dog for a 10-year-old girl with severe food allergies. Lee has an amazing talent of sensing when someone is particularly anxious and helping them calm down. She demonstrated unconditional love and empathy for this particular child. It was through these interactions that I knew Lee had to retire to this family. While she may not be working as hard physically as she did with me, she is serving such a critical role for this child.

Alette Coble-Temple, PsyD

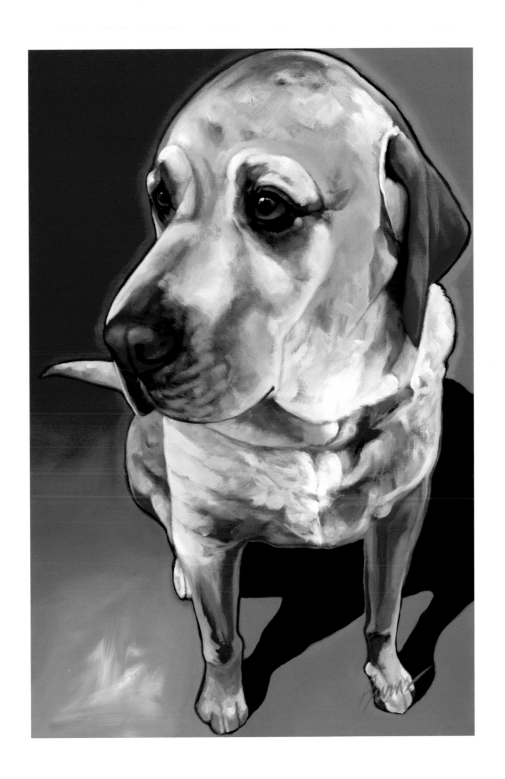

JOEY

Pet Therapy - Therapy Dogs International

As I scrolled down your email and the pictures of Joey emerged, I actually broke out into a sweat, and when I focused on the tight headshot picture, I just couldn't believe how real… almost breathing… this painting looked! Ron definitely has captured Joey, as Joey wore his heart in his expression with his beautiful eyes! I found myself with a grin from ear to ear. I was truly blessed to have a pet that emits this love.

Being a certified pet therapy dog was Joe's second career. Transforming from a racer to a pet gave him the opportunity to showcase his best talents. Joe visited rehabilitation centers, nursing homes, colleges, reading programs at libraries, appeared on a TV report, and shined at our pet store Meet & Greets. He was truly a majestic soul and loved people, and was loved by all people who met him, as well.

Joey made over 8 visits to Ground Zero.

Kathy Cartensen

BRETAGNE

Search and Rescue - Texas Task Force 1

Bretagne's career as a search dog began at the age of two, as a member of Texas Task Force 1, responding to the attacks on 9/11. Although she searched Ground Zero for ten days, she did not find any survivors. However, while waiting for her next assignment, she demonstrated an untrained skill for supporting the first responders on scene. Even in the midst of the chaos, the activity and the overwhelming sadness and stunning loss, she knew which firefighter needed her comfort, and she went to that person.

And today, at 14 years of age, a senior dog with silver highlights on her fur and retired from active search work, Bretagne brings that same "emotional intelligence" to her new job. Once a week, she spends several hours at an elementary school, where she is known as the "reading dog." First grade students greet her as she visits classrooms, where she "listens" attentively to them read to her. Sometimes she puts a paw on a student's hand, or curls up close to one of them. She also visits a classroom for students with emotional and behavioral challenges, such as autism. Not only does she provide a calming influence on the children, but she is quick to lean into a staff member who is having a rough day. That is Bretagne today, continuing a tradition of service that started many years ago.

Denise Corliss

LUCY

Search and Rescue - California Task Force 3

When I got Lucy she was a hardened professional with years of wilderness and disaster search experience. She had already survived two near-death experiences, one of which was a rattlesnake bite, incurred while on a wilderness search. She worked the OKC bombing with our Urban Search & Rescue team, CA Task Force 3.

At age 8 she injured her back leg and couldn't work on rubble for six months. In that six months she became a CA OES certified Human Remains Detection dog. Within a few months she had found a murder victim still buried 6 - 8 ft. deep in a landfill. Finding that lady's body put the bad guy away forever.

We trained and honed our skills as a team for years until we were called upon to work the World Trade Center in Sept. 2001 with CA TF4. She was incredible, finding her first human remains within five minutes of setting foot on the WTC site. In addition to her work locating the victims of this travesty, she would go up to firefighters, police officers and construction workers, offer little kisses of condolence and absorb their tears into her coat.

Following the crash of the Shuttle Columbia, Lucy was requested by NASA to fly to Texas to help locate the remains of our astronauts. She worked there for nine days as part of a massive team that eventually brought our astronauts home to their families.

I really miss working with/for Lucy. She was truly my partner in addition to being my best friend, accepting anything I did and loving me no matter what. Lucy died on August 4, 2006. Her last minutes were spent where she loved best, the rubble pile at the DART training site.

Lynne Engelbert

ABBY

Search and Rescue - FEMA

Abby and Debra bonded very quickly. They loved being together and practiced their search skills diligently. After only seven months, they attained Basic Certification for disaster search from the Federal Emergency Management Agency (FEMA). Three months later, they attained Advanced Certification and were considered one of the top canine/handler search teams in the nation.

On September 11th, 2001, their skills were put to the ultimate test when they were deployed to Ground Zero. The assignment was extremely dangerous and demanding, climbing over twisted metal and sharp, hot slabs of concrete, breathing in dust and smoke. But the teams were prepared for the challenge. The dogs are always eager to search: they enjoy it and even thrive on it! Debra and Abby searched the rubble in 12-hour shifts. At the end of the deployment, the teams were exhausted, but proud for having served their country and having met a profound physical and emotional challenge.

Abby retired after a lifetime of service to America, including deployments to the World Trade Center, the La Conchita mudslide, Hurricanes Katrina and Rita, and a Los Angeles train crash. This pioneering Search Dog passed away peacefully in her sleep, shortly before her 14th birthday. Abby has always and will continue to serve as a shining example of an exemplary working dog for generations of Search Dogs to come!

October 31, 1997 ~ September 24, 2011

Debra Tosch - Abby's Partner
Executive Director
National Disaster Search Dog Foundation

ABOUT THE ARTIST

It took an earthquake to help Ron Burns find his true calling. In the late 1980s he worked with high profile clients at his uber-successful design firm in Los Angeles. That all changed when the 1987 Whittier earthquake shook both his business and his life off its foundations.

Feeling the need to reprioritize and find something to feed the soul, Ron and his wife, Buff, moved to Sedona, Arizona where he began to paint, exploring various styles and subject matter until finally he found his passion painting vibrant portraits of their dogs.

"There's nothing subtle or understated about a pet's love, especially a dog's," says Ron. "It's heartfelt and full-strength and from the beginning the colors in my paintings – the green-apple colors, the fire-truck reds, the swimming-pool blues – really chose themselves."

Early on in his career, Ron started each portrait with the eyes and he continues that technique today.

"Their eyes hold nothing back, whether it's love or heartbreak or admiration. Every portrait begins there; they have to because from there all the life and personality radiates outward," he says.

After Ron's initial series of paintings of his own "kids," he started visiting animal shelters and taking photos of other dogs and cats to use as models. After selling portraits of these images, he returned a percentage of proceeds back to support the shelters.

Through his charity work, Ron has helped to raise millions of dollars across the country to support animal shelters and animal-support nonprofits. This led to being named Artist-in-Residence with The Humane Society of the United States.

His work is in high demand with collectors, private galleries, and museum collections. He has been featured on CNN, Good Morning America, and Extreme Makeover: Home Edition as well as in the pages of Forbes, New York Daily News, San Francisco Chronicle and many other media outlets. Ron has painted portraits of dogs for celebrities, captains of industry and collectors worldwide.

When the world changed on September 11 Ron focused on painting what he calls 'hero dogs' – canines who assist humans in amazing ways as bomb detection, search and rescue, and therapy dogs. He is deeply honored that his painting of Sirius, the explosive detection dog, who died in the collapse of Tower Two at the World Trade Center on September 11, 2001, is included in the permanent collection of the 9/11 Memorial Museum.

"Their eyes hold nothing back, whether it's love or heartbreak or admiration."

Ron Burns